Get Paid To Help Offline Businesses Get Online!

Offline Goldmine

LEGAL NOTICE:

The Publisher has strived to be as accurate and complete as possible in the creation of this report, notwithstanding the fact that he does not warrant or represent at any time that the contents within are accurate due to the rapidly changing nature of the Internet.

While all attempts have been made to verify information provided in this publication, the Publisher assumes no responsibility for errors, omissions, or contrary interpretation of the subject matter herein.

Any perceived slights of specific persons, peoples, or organizations are unintentional.

Disclaimer

Please note the information contained within this document are for educational purposes only.

Every attempt has been made to provide accurate, up to date and reliable complete information no warranties of any kind are expressed or implied. Readers acknowledge that the author is not engaging in rendering legal, financial or professional advice.

By reading any document, the reader agrees that under no circumstances are we responsible for any losses, direct or indirect, that are incurred as a result of use of the information contained within this document, including - but not limited to errors, omissions, or inaccuracies.

Table Of Contents

OFFLINE GOLDMINE INTRODUCTION 5
CREATING YOUR BUSINESS PLAN 10
    SITE BUILDING AND RENOVATION 16
    HOSTING 17
    MAINTENANCE 17
    SEO AND TRAFFIC 18
    EMAIL MARKETING 18
BUILDING YOUR CLIENT BASE 20
    WAYS TO LOCATE CLIENTS 20
        Walk-Ins 20
        Cold Calling 20
        Flyers 21
        Direct Mail Marketing 21
        Business Cards 21
        Yellow Pages 21
        Chamber of Commerce Meetings 22
        Seminars and Speaking Engagements 22
        Newspaper Advertising 22
        Look Online! 23
SOLIDIFYING THE SALE 24
    CONTRACTS 25
BUILDING YOUR OUTSOURCE TEAM 27
PRICING YOUR SERVICES 31
    FLAT RATE VS. HOURLY 32
    STARTING POINTS 34
BUMPS IN THE ROAD 37
THE PAYMENT PROCESS 39
FINAL WORDS: CONCLUSION 42

Offline Goldmine Introduction

With the Internet, many of have learned to develop profitable businesses that involve little start up costs, fewer production costs, and very little if any overhead.

We all got caught up on just how easy it was to build a business online, and having the global outreach to be able to connect with thousands, if not millions of potential customers all over the world certainly made us sit up and pay attention.

But just how easy is it to build a successful online company?

In every market and industry, you're swarmed with competition. Even ranking in Google for your chosen keywords can be a time consuming and frustrating process.

That's not to say that you can't make a living online with a website and product line of your own, you can, but we've become so narrow minded with believing that in order to become a successful entrepreneur, our main focus should always start and end with the Internet.

It's simply not entirely true.

Think of all the countless businesses in your local area.

How many of those people would benefit by having a web presence?

Now, think again about the sheer number of mom & pop shops that don't have a presence and calculate how much money you could make if you were the bridge that connected their business with the world wide web.

When you think about how many customers are right there at your fingertips, and you begin to focus on how you can build a profitable business just by helping them expand their own business, you will quickly discover the quick and easy recipe to success.

With offline business there is far less competition. Unlike online markets where you are forced to elbow your way through the massive crowds just to get your food in the industry, with offline marketing, you are your only competition.

There is likely to be less resistance as well since these companies see you as their connection to broadening their outreach and taking their business to a whole new level.

Plus, by being able to connect with someone personally rather than having to outsource or hire the work out to an anonymous company or service online, you will be able to develop sincere relationships with your clients who will come to rely on you for helping their business grow in a whole new way.

But it's certainly not new to you right?

You already know how lucrative having an online presence can be and even if you don't know how to do all of the different services that you will begin to offer local businesses, you already know exactly how to outsource this to seasoned professionals and freelancers.

You know of the marketplaces, the forums, the freelance communities and all you have to do is secure the project - pass the work over to a freelancer - and cash in.

Your job? Managing the project. It's never been so easy to make money on and offline.

The Offline Insider guide was written by a group of us who decided to give these strategies a real shot. We decided to focus 2 months of our time on penetrating the offline market to see just how viable it really was.

I'll be honest with you, none of us really expected that our business would grow so quickly, in fact, we were all looking at the process as an interesting experiment more than a life and business changing endeavour.

What we discovered however is that there are literally hundreds of businesses in every town and city across the world that have yet to connect to the global outreach that the Internet provides.

While many of these companies know that they SHOULD get "online", few of them have any idea how.

Worse, it's extremely intimidating for these businesses to even consider hiring a service provider online to develop their websites and help them get their message out to their market because they simply don't know whether the price quotes they are given are reasonable, or whether they truly need specific services that are being offered in a carousel of up-sells and ridiculous offers that will never truly help their business grow.

But when someone comes along who is available to them locally, who seems to have a solid business plan created, and who appears to genuinely want to help their business expand and reach out to new customers, they suddenly start to feel hopeful again, to envision how much larger their business could be when given this fresh new online audience.

You will be able to generate more interest and build a larger client list in a short amount of time than nearly any other opportunity available to you, just by connecting with local businesses and offering them something they know they already need, an online presence.

The Offline Goldmine will show you exactly how to build a profitable business following simple, yet proven strategies that will solidify your place in your local area and help you generate ongoing business by taking offline businesses - online.

Let's get started.

Creating Your Business Plan

Creating your business plan is the first step in being able to connect with offline clients.

You don't need to spend a lot of money developing your service plans, and you really don't need to even rent out office space when you are just getting started.

Most of your meetings will take place at your clients business, but you can also communicate through phone regularly once you have sealed the deal.

But first, do you remember how difficult everything seemed to be when you first started building an online business?

Remember how frustrating and outright daunting building that first blog or website felt?

If you had someone come along and offer you an affordable solution where you didn't have to lift a finger and they would set up a fully functional, optimized website for you, wouldn't you have considered taking them up on that incredible deal?

You need to keep that mindset when building your business plan and service offers.

These offline businesses understand how important it is that they build an online presence, but many of them won't understand exactly WHAT they need.

You also want to come down to the beginner level with terminology as well.

If you approach a local business who is not familiar with the business terms used online like SEO or PPC, you will find it harder to land the project, because these people will only end up confused and unsure as to whether they are 'cut out' for this whole complicated online thing.

You need to simplify it, to thoroughly explain the benefits of every service that you are offering and in the event that one of your services doesn't fit a client's business, it should never be part of the presentation.

That means that every service offer you present to a potential client needs to be custom tailored to what you believe their business needs in order to expand their outreach and maximize their profits.

Catering to offline businesses involves far more than just developing their websites, although this is usually the first step in a variety of service agreements that you can build with each client.

But think outside of the obvious first step. After their website is developed, what next?

What else can you offer that will make a genuine difference in their ability to promote their brand and company online?

What about traffic generation strategies?

Optimizing their websites for the search engines?

Generating back-links to their website?

Developing online promotional material and creatives or incorporating an affiliate program to help them generate fresh leads?

You really need to evaluate the business first, before contacting them to determine exactly how to approach them in such a way that they will feel as though you have taken a personal interest in helping their business expand because you have done your homework.

You know their business, you understand their concerns, you know what they want and need and can deliver it to them.

You may be concerned that this process will become overly time consuming and in reality, it can be chiselled down so that it only takes a few hours to customize each presentation for every local business you intend on approaching.

You first develop your service listing. This will include every service that you plan to offer to a variety of businesses. You also develop your price structure and overall business plan.

Then, with each new business that you communicate with, you adjust this service offer to suit their needs, cutting out what is not needed or adding in a handful of services that would directly benefit each company.

So this is where you need to begin, by defining your service offers, assigning price points to each service and ironing out the small details.

You can also expand on your service offers or modify them later on if needed, but your first step is to write down everything that you believe you could offer to a local business, explore the industry for average prices for each service offer, and create a solid business plan that you can use when approaching each company.

This doesn't have to be time consuming, you can simply dedicate a few days to evaluating the market and researching what other people are currently offering to online businesses and then adapt this information into creating a rock solid, irresistible offline offer.

Here are a few ideas on services that you could offer:

Web Development
Developing their websites and blogs, SILO structures, email campaigns.

Online Marketing
Sub categories: Link Building, Email Marketing, Feeder Sites, Search engine optimization

Training
After you develop their online business, you could offer personal training services where you show them how to maintain their

websites, update their pages, etc.

Updates & Maintenance

You could charge a monthly recurring fee to update their websites or blogs, to email their clients or manage their mailing lists.

Promotional Material Creation

You could offer to integrate an affiliate program, provide affiliate creatives and so on.

Content Development

Create articles for marketing purposes, website article updates, brochures, press releases etc.

You need to create a service page on a professionally designed website that clearly outlines the different service packages you are offering, along with an estimated price structure, or even better, giving visitors the opportunity to fill in a form in order to request a custom quote.

This is a critical step of the process, even if you intend on advertising your services entirely offline, because once you've snagged a few new customers, they might want to verify that you, yourself have an online presence and know exactly what you're talking about.

If you are intending on offering design services, consider creating a sample portfolio that showcases designs that you have completed for past clients, or if you intend on offering online marketing campaigns, you should outline exactly what is included with each package as well as any available case studies you have at your disposal, showcasing exactly what you can do.

If you are planning to outsource the majority of the work, also keep in mind the costs associated with hiring freelancers and make sure that you will be able to generate a profit based on different price structures.

Once you have begun to work with a handful of offline businesses, you will have a better idea as to any price resistance and can adjust your price plan accordingly.

Here are other services to consider:

Site Building and Renovation
Obviously, the most common service will be building or revamping a website. Many companies don't have a website at all, and a lot of those that do have sites that were built by amateurs and are too hard to update.

I recommend using WordPress to build the website for most companies. It's flexible, easy to use, and makes it very easy for the client to update if he doesn't want to pay you a monthly fee to do so.

Hosting

Every website must have hosting, and there are a couple of ways you can make money from your clients with it. The most obvious is to simply host their site yourself and charge them a monthly fee for it.

If you're not up for the responsibility of hosting your clients' sites yourself, you can sign up as an affiliate for various web hosting companies and send your clients to them through an affiliate link.

Companies like HostGator pay up to $100 or more for every customer you refer, so this could be quite lucrative if you get a lot of clients.

Maintenance

Some websites require very little maintenance, and others must be updated with sales and specials or inventory on a very regular basis.

Additionally, SEO may also require some ongoing maintenance in the form of tweaking pages and getting backlinks. It takes a bit of work to get to the top and stay there.

These are services you could charge a monthly fee for. You could ask your client what type of updates they would need, and then price your service accordingly.

SEO and Traffic

Obviously, the websites you build will need traffic, which means you will need to do some search engine optimization and other traffic work.

You'll need to generate backlinks for the site, get the company listed in various online directories including Google's local search, and more.

You can charge for the initial setup and optimization, as well as any ongoing monthly services like backlink building. This could be a great additional source of income each month.

Email Marketing

One service every business needs but few actually have is email marketing. Most companies that build websites don't offer this service to their clients, so even companies that already have websites aren't usually using it.

It's also an unbelievably important tool. Every business relies on repeat business to sustain it.

If customers don't come back, a business can't survive very long, especially in smaller markets.

Using email marketing, a company can keep customers coming back again and again.

They can send out messages for special offers, coupons, announcements, updates, and special events. This keeps customers reminded that they exist, and also bring customers back in to the location to take advantage of special offers.

You could offer to simply set up the email marketing system for the client, or you could charge a monthly fee for managing their email system each month. This is yet another potential source of recurring income.

In the next chapter, we will take a look at the different ways of reaching out to these businesses and building your client list.

Building Your Client Base

Almost any local business could benefit from your services. Even a small local convenience store could bring in more business by having a website and email list!

No customer is too small to have an online presence, so don't worry about trying to approach "just the right type of business". In fact, any business is the right type of business for this system!

Ways to Locate Clients
There are many ways to potentially find clients. We're going to look at some of the best ways to find local businesses that might be receptive to your services.

Walk-Ins
One of the best ways to find business is by just walking in and asking to speak to the manager.

Talking face to face is a great way to establish trust.

Cold Calling
Many people prefer to call businesses rather than hitting the streets and going door to door. It's less effective than walking in, but it's easier, especially if you don't have good transportation.

Flyers

Flyers can be very effective if you word them well. Don't focus your marketing material on building websites, but on bringing the company more business.

Direct Mail Marketing

If you've ever received an advertisement in the forum of a sales letter or postcard in the mail, (and who hasn't?) then you've seen direct mail marketing in action. A good direct mail campaign can be very effective.

Business Cards

Some people get a great deal of business simply by giving a business card to every business owner they come in contact with.

Get a haircut? Give the salon owner a card. Just got your car repaired? Don't forget to slip your card to the owner of the shop!

Yellow Pages

Start by browsing through the yellow pages of your local directory searching for start up business or mom & pop shops that could use your help. You can also use online search engines to determine newly registered businesses in your local area.

Chamber of Commerce Meetings

If your area has a local Chamber of Commerce or other business organization, be sure to attend as many of their meetings as you can.

Networking with other business owners is a fantastic way to pick up business, as well as referrals.

Seminars and Speaking Engagements

One extremely effective way to find clients is to speak at seminars and other local events where you know business owners will be. If you can't find an event to speak at, set one up!

If you arrange a free seminar on how businesses can use the internet to get more business, you're sure to find a few people who will want your services after hearing your "expert" speech.

Newspaper Advertising

Don't forget about the power of your local newspaper. An ad in the "Business Services" section is inexpensive, but may not be as effective as a larger ad. But either type of add should bring in enough business to justify the cost if your ad is well written.

Look Online!

Regardless if your client already has an existing website, it may be in need of an overhaul or revision.

Use the major search engines to find both local and distance businesses that need some work.

You could also browse through online business directories and marketplaces including www.clickbank.com and www.cj.com to find online businesses that could be improved through both web design, sales funnel, sales copy, list building, traffic campaigns and more!

Solidifying The Sale

After you've found a potential client and they seem interested, it's time to close the sale.

This in one of the hardest parts for most people, because the majority of people have a fear of rejection. When you're worried about being rejected, you're reluctant to ask for the sale.

It's very important to remember the A-B-C of sales. Always Be Closing. Everything you say and do should lead up to closing the deal. Otherwise, your time is wasted.

Don't be afraid to ask for the sale. Once you've made your case and shown the lead you know what you're talking about, it's time to close.

Consider the following phrases when discussing projects with potential clients:

- "So when should I get started?"
- "How would you like to pay for the service?"
- "I could get started today if you're ready."
- "Why don't we get started on this right away."

If you don't say things like this, most people will not volunteer.

Sometimes people will be so excited that they will voluntarily offer the sale, but generally people will avoid it. You must ask!

Contracts

I don't generally recommend asking a client to sign a contract for minor work, but if you're looking at making significant money you might want to consider this.

You could have an attorney draw up a general agreement that you could use over and over just by filling in the blanks.

If you aren't being paid up front, it's vital to get a contract. If the company decides to renege on your deal and you have no written contract, it will be difficult (if not impossible) to get your money.

When it comes to building your client list, and growing your online business by contacting offline businesses, you need to adapt a very different mindset than you might be familiar with in online business.

<u>You are not SELLING anything!</u>

Instead, your job is to help business owners understand how their business will improve through your services.

All you are going to do is talk to potential customers, get their feedback as to what is important to them and then explain to them exactly how an online presence will benefit their overall business.

You want to thoroughly evaluate their existing business, determine what they are already doing to market their business offline and simply show them how much more exposure they will gain, by taking their business online.

When you switch your mindset so that you are merely discussing, responding and helping people improve their business, you will find it a heck of a lot easier to recruit clients.

Building Your Outsource Team

Since you will likely want to outsource the majority of the work involved with each project, it's important to become familiar with online freelance communities and to build a profile that will welcome new freelancers into your business plan.

To start, there are dozens of freelance communities online but I personally recommend setting up an account at the following websites:

http://www.elance.com
http://www.Guru.com
http://www.Scriptlance.com (especially if you are offering any custom programming services)

For content providers, you could also include:

http://www.WarriorForum.com (see "Warriors for Hire")

http://www.Workaholics4Hire.com
Your job as a middleman between a company and the professionals who can take their vision and make it a reality involves you being able to effectively manage each project carefully, and to ensure that

project deadlines are met and that your client receives consistent updates and progress reports.

You never want to leave a client in the dark, especially if they have never hired a service provider like you before.

You want to always be available to them should they have any questions or require a bit more help understanding the process.

The easier you make the entire process for them, the easier it will be secure ongoing work from each company.

When setting up your freelance team, you really want to save money by hiring people only as you need them.

There are many over-zealous entrepreneurs who saw the potential in going offline who quickly developed a massive freelance team thinking that they would need to secure as many "on call" developers as possible.

Not only will this become very distracting and time consuming keeping in communication with a large team of freelancers but it will also increase your costs significantly.

Only hire freelancers, as you need them based on each project that you acquire.

You will begin to build relationships with the freelancers that you do hire over time, and it's likely that you will be able to start contacting people directly whenever you need some quick help without having to post projects on the public freelance communities.

The transaction process would work this like:

- You collect payment from your client - you THEN secure the freelancer.

- Offer the freelancer a deposit payment upfront with the remainder payable only on completion of the work (unless you know the freelancer personally or they have a solid reputation and history in the field).

Offer services on an individual basis as well as part of a collective business package, showing the benefits and savings if a client chooses a full feature package over individual services.

You always want to highlight the savings should a company hire you for an array of services, rather than on a per project basis.

You'll find that clients will be far more likely to book you for numerous projects if they believe that it will save them money in the long run so it's your job to always emphasize the savings and benefits.

You can do this by offering new clients coupons or discount certificates that they can use to place orders for different services, or to use in the future once the original project has been completed.

And remember, there is no service that you can't offer to clients.

If you feel that they would benefit from a specific service, or they begin asking for additional services that are not part of your original business plan, just take the order - hire a professional freelancer - and use your online connections to increase your own income while being able to cater to any request.

Pricing Your Services

One thing a lot of people struggle with is how to price their services. There is no one-size-fits-all approach, as your price will depend on many different factors.

For example, pricing would be affected by:

- The current state of the economy
- Your location, and how much competition exists.
- How much you really need to make to cover expenses.
- The type of service being offered, and time allocated to each project.

Perhaps the most important factor has to do with you personally. Ultimately, you need to make enough to make it worth your time to perform this service.

Determine what the absolute lowest price you would be willing to accept would be. Try to price your services at twice that rate.

That way, if you have to come down in price to get the client, you'll have a lot of leeway for negotiation before you reach your "lowest price".

You'll also have to take into consideration your location. If there are a lot of web design firms around your area, many websites may already have a website.

If your competition is keen on internet marketing, they may also be offering some of the same services. You may have to price competitively in order to gain business.

The economy is also a major factor. As much as it sucks, you may have to price your services far lower than you normally would if the economy is especially bad.

When the economy is suffering, businesses aren't making as much money, so they wouldn't be able to pay you as much as they normally would, however by acquiring their business early on, when the economy picks up, you can begin to increase your prices accordingly.

Flat Rate vs. Hourly
Whether you charge a flat rate or hourly rate is up to you, but I recommend charging a flat rate for services.

You may have a hard time convincing businesses to pay you an hourly rate, and you don't want to upset the client by taking longer than anticipated and charging more than your initial quote.

When you charge a flat rate, you'll need to draw up a detailed plan of action, including everything your client expects.

This way you're protected if the client later wants something that wasn't agreed to, and the client is covered if you accidentally forget something that was agreed to.

If the client wants changes after you've delivered what was promised, you may want to charge an additional fee for this.

Don't get caught up in endless revisions. They will monopolize your time and leave you falling behind with other projects as well as reducing the actual profits.

Don't forget about charging monthly fees for ongoing work as well. Services including hosting and regular website maintenance updates can be great sources of recurring income, so make sure to include these in your service offers.

You may want to charge your client for several months in advance at a discount rate as well. That way, the client doesn't have to worry about that payment for a while, is able to see the long term savings, and you don't have to worry about non-payment.

Note: You should always offer some sort of discount if you are going to charge in advance.

For example, if you were going to charge $50 per month for a service, you might charge only $45 or even $40 per month if they pay 6 or 12 months in advance.

Starting Points

Some people want a good starting point for pricing, so I'm going to give you some numbers you can use.

Just keep in mind that pricing will vary greatly based on many factors, including special requests from the client, the client's industry, and what type of site the client needs.

Obviously a fully functional e-commerce store would cost much more than a simple five page website, so keep that in mind. These are just rough guidelines to get you started!

- 5 Page Website - $250-$500
- Email Marketing Setup - $150-$300
- Hosting - $5-$25 per month
- Initial SEO for a 5 Page Website - $150-$300
- Monthly SEO and Backlinking - $25-$100 per month
- Monthly Email Marketing - $25-$200
- Monthly Site Maintenance - $50-$150

Remember, these are just rough guidelines!

For example, monthly email marketing could be anywhere from $25 for one short email per month up to several hundred dollars if you are expected to send several messages per week, or if you have to craft long and very detailed messages.

Ultimately, your pricing will be highly dependent on what you feel you need to make for each service, and what exactly the client expects.

Consider all options when creating your price structure.

A client who pays you a recurring fee each month to host his or her website, and an additional fee to update it is far more valuable than a one-off project, and so you should consider adjusting your prices to offer them a feasible discount in order to retain them over the long run.

Bumps In The Road

You will almost certainly run into difficult clients from time to time. Unfortunately, they are a part of doing business.

Most clients will be pleasant to work with, but we've all run into a handful who are simply confused or overwhelmed by the whole process, are concerned over progress, or simply need a bit more guidance in order to fully understand what you are offering, and how you are helping them.

Remember as well that not everyone is going to see the work that went on behind the scenes.

If they have no experience developing online businesses, it's likely that you will want to take your time in explaining the process, what you and your team have been doing, and why it's an important part in the growth of their online exposure.

For the most part, you should try to work with clients to make sure they are happy every step of the way, and to do your part in being understanding by putting yourself in their position.

Remember, these people trust in you, they have agreed to let you manage an important part of their business; their online presence and you need to be sincere in communicating with them every step of the way.

Remember, clients who are very happy will potentially refer other clients to you in the future. This could mean a great deal of business.

The Payment Process

With every client that you take on, you will want to create an agreement that clearly explains your obligations as well as any monetary obligations associated with the deal.

Some clients may pay you upfront, which is always best, and at the very least you should require a deposit of the overall service cost.

Most businesses, however, will expect to be able to pay you after you're finished with the work. In fact, many businesses are used to paying on a Net-30 basis, which means they receive an invoice for most of the goods and services they buy which they can pay up to 30 days later.

This is tough when you're a small business. Waiting 30 days to be paid can put you into serious financial trouble when you're just starting out especially when you have to pay the freelancers that you have hired to complete the work.

To avoid this, you may want to offer a hefty discount for clients who pay in advance.

Remember when I said you should charge double the lowest price you're really willing to accept?

This is important, because when you're negotiating with a client who is hesitant to pay in advance, you can use that leeway to offer a big discount if payment is made upfront. Again always highlight the savings and benefits to your client every step of the way.

Offer a 10%, 25%, even 50% discount if your client will pay in advance.

If you are new service provider, you might find it difficult to convince businesses to pay the entire bill without seeing results, however as you build your client portfolio, you will be in the position to require a larger upfront deposit or the entire amount.

You could accept 50% upfront payment, which would be your lowest possible price, and if you were never paid the balance it wouldn't matter so much.

Ultimately you would at least be paid your minimum amount that would cover your freelance costs and your time.

While you should always leave room for negotiation, with your price structure, you never want to walk away feeling as if you under-cut yourself.

Notes: If you can, hire a lawyer who can create a basic agreement for you that you can re-purpose and use with each client.

With a contract that identifies the responsibilities or obligations of both parties, you will be in the position to seek compensation in the event that your client fails to complete payment.

Final Words: Conclusion

Building a relationship with each client is exceptionally important and the more you work towards communicating with each client on a regular basis, by involving them in the entire process as much as possible and by showing them exactly how you are able to improve their business, you will be able to position yourself so that you never have to seek out project work again – they will come to you!

Take a real genuine interest in the businesses that you work with. After all, you should sincerely want to help them maximize their outreach and their bottom line because the greater progress and improvement they see from your work, the more likely they will come to you again and again.

Also keep in mind that referrals will make up a very large part of your client base, and it always begins with a single client.

Remain focused with your business plan and never give up!

While it may take a bit of time for you to build a client list, if you stay persistent and do your best to offer each business a customized service proposal that showcases the many ways that you can help them improve their business, you WILL succeed.

Remember, it's about you HELPING them – not SELLING to them.

Offer your services to those who genuinely need it, work hard, be fierce, and never stop believing in yourself. The possibilities are truly endless!

To your off and online success,

Your Name,

www.ingramcontent.com/pod-product-compliance
Lightning Source LLC
LaVergne TN
LVHW011900060526
838200LV00054B/4453